130+ PUMPKIN CARVING STENCILS

To watch a video tutorial showing how to use the carving stencils please scan the above QR code.

Or visit: bit.ly/CarvingTut

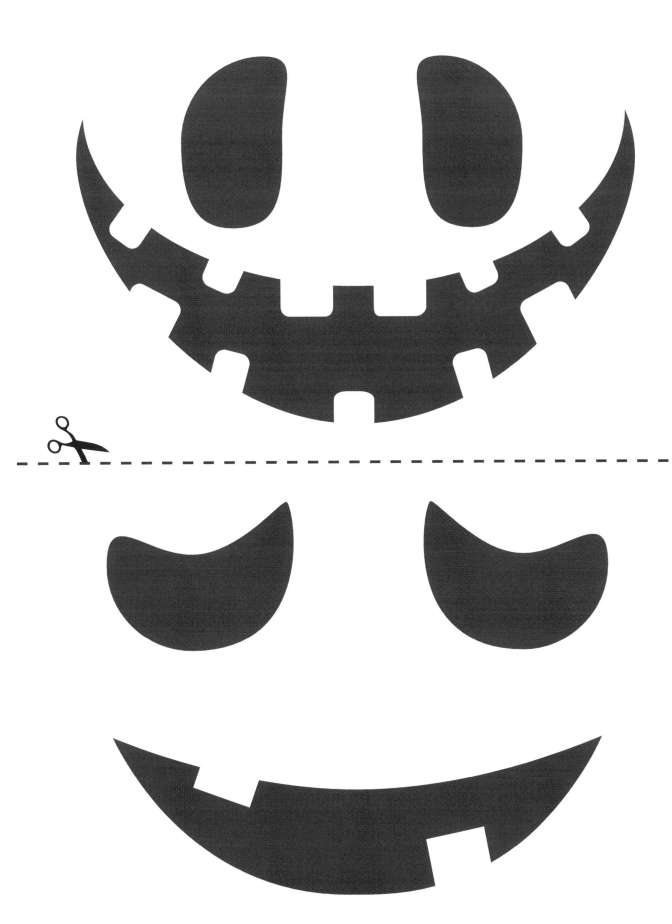

✂ -

✂ -

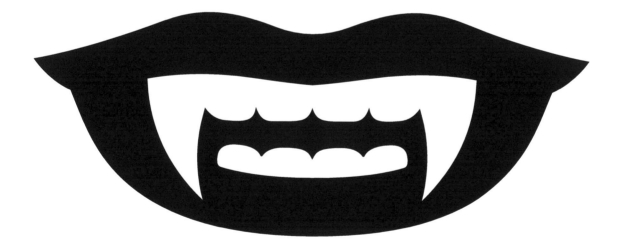

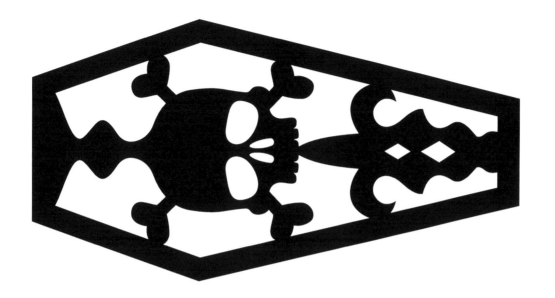
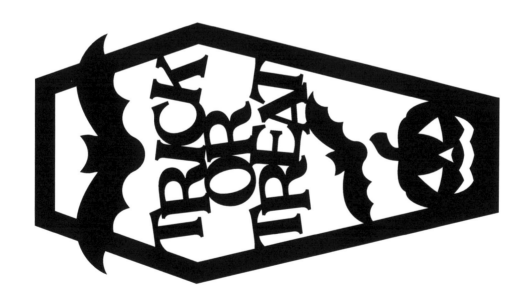

TRICK OR TREAT

BOO

BOO

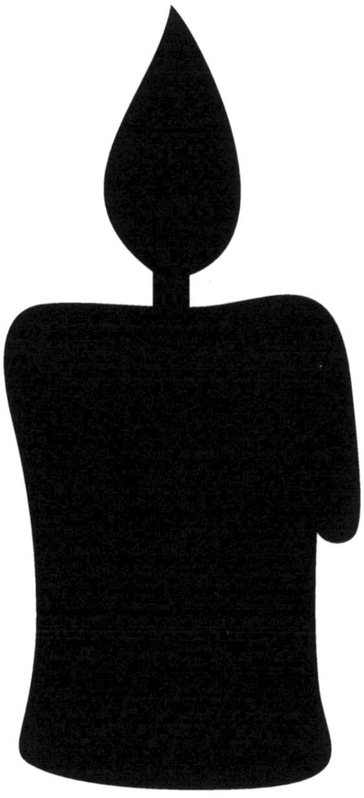

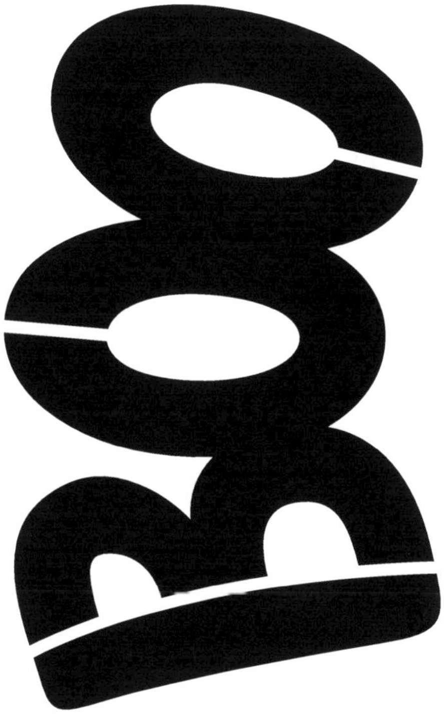
BOO

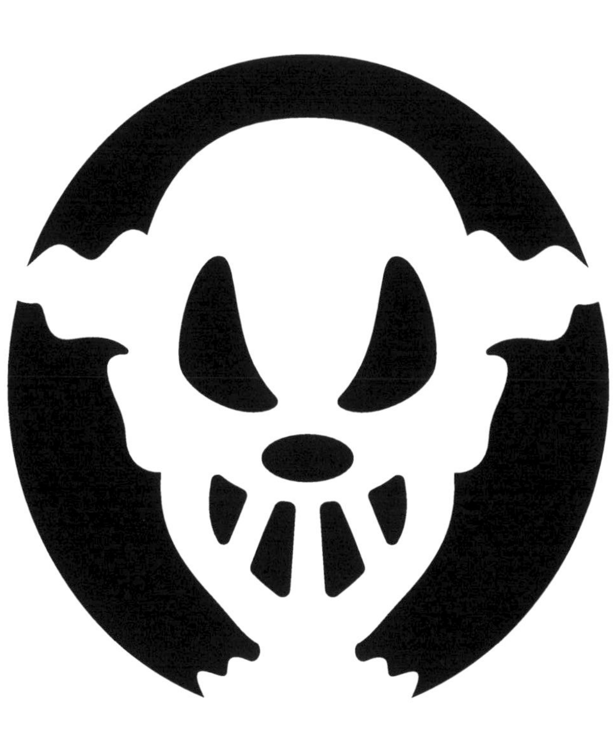

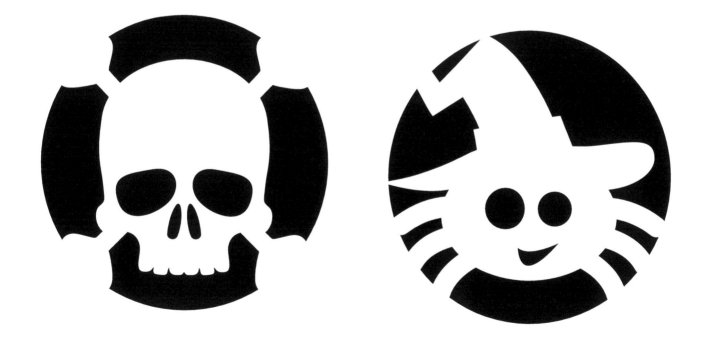

Made in the USA
Middletown, DE
16 October 2023

40888951R00091